PUZZLE IT OUT!
LOGIC
PUZZLES

BY PAUL VIRR AND LISA REGAN
ILLUSTRATED BY AMANDA ENRIGHT

WINDMILL
BOOKS

Published in 2020 by Windmill Books,
an Imprint of Rosen Publishing
29 East 21st Street, New York, NY 10010

Cataloging-in-Publication Data

Names: Virr, Paul. | Regan, Lisa.
Title: Logic puzzles / Paul Virr and Lisa Regan.
Description: New York : Windmill Books, 2020. | Series: Puzzle it out! | Includes glossary and index.
Identifiers: ISBN 9781538392041 (pbk.) | ISBN 9781538392065 (library bound) | ISBN 9781538392058 (6 pack)
Subjects: LCSH: Logic puzzles--Juvenile literature.
Classification: LCC GV1493.V577 2019 | DDC 793.74--dc2

Manufactured in the United States of America

CPSIA Compliance Information: Batch BS19WM: For Further Information contact Rosen Publishing, New York, New York at 1-800-237-9932

CONTENTS

SLEEPY KITTENS

The kittens are tired! They like to snuggle up with three kittens in a basket, so how many baskets would you need for all of them?

Odd One Out

Count the legs on each creature and point to the odd one out in each set.

Number Crunching!

Big Bunny ate two carrots for lunch,
but how many did his friends eat?
Read the clues and work it out!

Cleaning Windows

Each worker cleans the shape of window shown on their clothes. Which one cleans the most windows?

Percy's Potion

It is in a round bottle.
It has bubbles in it.
It isn't blue.

8

Home with Mr. Wolf

Which of these houses belongs to Mr. Wolf?

It has blue curtains.
It has flowers outside.

Treasure Seekers

Which island has treasure buried on it? Use the clues to work it out.

There are huts on it.

It has more than two palm trees.

Dog Tricks

Bruno likes to run around every tree twice. What is the total number of times he will run around a tree in this park?

Lost and Found

Baby Bunnikins wants the flower that adds up to 9. Which flower does she want?

5 + 4

2 + 6

3 + 3

3 + 7

Hello There!

This koala's age is half the number of leaves around him. How old is the koala?

Achoo!

Leo the lion sneezes 3 times every
time he comes near a flower.
How many times will he sneeze here?

Mrs. Wishy's Wash

How many pairs of things can you find on Mrs. Wishy's clothesline?

SLIP AND SLIDE

START

Fred and Maisie are going down the super slide.
Use your finger to find the best way to the swimming
pool without hitting a tree or a rock.

FINISH

Monkey Puzzle

Help this monkey to find her way home. Her tree is the one that equals 11.

18 - 7 = ?

20 - 7 = ?

14 - 7 = ?

15 - 7 = ?

19 - 7 = ?

Pizza Puzzle

Everyone's ordering pizza!
Help the waiter figure out how many slices
to give each hungry customer.

Spy School

Welcome to Spy School! Crack the code to get to your class. You need the door with the code that equals 5.

Sparkly Gems

Look at these sparkly bracelets!
Which bracelet would give you the most points?

● = 1 point   ■ = 2 points
⬡ = 3 points   ▲ = 4 points

Busy Bees

Each bee visits a different flower before heading back to the hive. How many flowers are not visited by these bees?

Apple Picking

Help the farmer pick her apples.
How many red apples are there?
Are there more green apples or red apples?

Happy Hens

Each happy hen lays eggs that match
its feathers. Which hen has laid the most?
How many eggs will the farmer collect?

HOME SWEET HOME

These aliens have lost their way! Help them find their home. It's the planet with the most craters.

Easy Cheesy!

If each mouse eats the biggest piece of cheese on their plate, how many holes are left in the remaining two pieces?

Spot Spotting

How many groups of bugs with the same number of spots can you find? Get out your magnifying glass, and take a closer look!

ANSWERS

Page 4 Sleepy Kittens

You would need 4 baskets for the kittens.

Page 5 Odd One Out

Hedgehog
Ant
Butterfly
Bat

Page 6 Number Crunching!

Black Bunny ate 5 carrots.
Red Bunny ate 3 carrots.
White Bunny ate 1 carrot.
Yellow Bunny ate 5 carrots.

Page 7 Cleaning Windows

The worker cleaning the square
windows cleans the most.

Page 8 Percy's Potion

Page 9 Home with Mr. Wolf

Page 10 Treasure Seekers

Page 11 Dog Tricks

There are 2 trees in the park, so Bruno will run around a tree 4 times in total.

Page 12 Lost and Found

Page 13 Hello There!

The koala is 5 years old.

Page 14 Achoo!

Leo will sneeze 9 times.

Page 15 Mrs. Wishy's Wash

There are 5 pairs of things on the clothesline.

Page 16-17 Slip and Slide

Page 18 Monkey Puzzle

Page 19 Pizza Puzzles

The first customer needs 2 slices.
The second customer needs 1 slice.
The third customer needs 4 slices.

Page 20 Spy School

The green door adds up to 5.

Page 21 Sparkly Gems

The bracelet with 4 triangles would give you the most points.

Page 22 Busy Bees

Three flowers are not visited.

Page 23 Apple Picking

There are 10 red apples. There are more green apples than red apples.

Page 24 Happy Hens

The brown hen has laid 9 eggs, which is the most. The farmer will collect 21 eggs.

Page 25 Home Sweet Home

The green planet has the most craters.

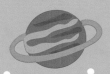

Page 26 Easy Cheesy

a = 7 holes

b = 7 holes

c = 9 holes

Page 27 Spot Spotting

There are 4 groups of bugs.

GLOSSARY

bugs Small insects.

code Letters or numbers with a secret meaning.

craters Holes in the ground.

gems Jewels.

hive A bee's nest, or home.

spy Someone who watches secretly.

INDEX

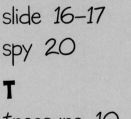